To: my daughter Melissa.

xMas 2011

mum

THE PROMISE

Unlock Your Potential

A new chapter in your life
is about to begin

Sandy Money

AuthorHouse™
1663 Liberty Drive
Bloomington, IN 47403
www.authorhouse.com
Phone: 1-800-839-8640

© 2010 Sandy Money. All rights reserved.

No part of this book may be reproduced, stored in a retrieval system, or transmitted by any means without the written permission of the author.

First published by AuthorHouse 11/17/2010

ISBN: 978-1-4520-0148-7 (e)
ISBN: 978-1-4520-0147-0 (sc)

Library of Congress Control Number: 2010903963

Printed in the United States of America
Bloomington, Indiana

This book is printed on acid-free paper.

Cover Photo by: Raquel Robinson

Dedication

I want to express my gratitude to God for allowing me to write this book and for the inspiration that was given to me, and to my three wonderful children.

Mary. I am grateful to have a daughter like you. Thank you for believing in me, for your encouraging words; whenever I had doubts about myself, you gave me hope by your beautiful smile and kind words, which gave me reasons to continue living.

Bryan. God knew that I needed a son like you to help me grow and become my best. I am grateful for the way you are, for your desire to become productive and successful. You are always looking to become your best. I admire your leadership. You are a blessing in my life.

Michael. I am very grateful for your gentle heart; you have always been the peacemaker. Thank you for your kind words, which always let me know that I was the best mother in the world to you, and you didn't wish for any other mother.

I want you to know that those kind words gave me strength and courage to face the challenges in my life.

Mr. Al Thomas. A special thank you to my mentor for teaching me that residual income creates happiness.

Mr. Nile Leatham. Thank you from the bottom of my heart to my spiritual mentor for teaching me that with Christ, I can do anything.

Julie Masters. Thank you to my beautiful and special friend for being there for me, especially through my tough times (my heavenly sister).

Phil Moulton. Thank you to my greatest friend. You are the best listener, because you are always there, ready to listen to my complaining. You are like a brother to me.

Thank you to the United States of America, which I love with all of my heart.

With all my love,

Sandy Money

About the Book

The human mind is like a parachute;
It only works if it's open!
I am not telling you what to do or how to do it;
I am just reminding you of the things you already know.
Be grateful for your life, the beauty of the earth, our country, and all the other things you can think of.
Believe you can learn to be great at anything and do anything that you set your mind to.
Change: make that change in the areas that you think are important to you.
Desire, followed by action, is the key to success!
Remember that the universe will give you only what you ask for.
Study, learn, and teach; most of all, have fun!

Be great!
Sandy Money

About the Author

Since I was very young I had a dream to be a part of this great country. I always knew that someday I would go to the United States of America. I have achieved that dream and many others. I came to the United States at the age of twenty-five. I didn't know anybody and spoke very little English, but I did have desire and an attitude for success to live the American dream!

Since I've been here, I've been given wonderful opportunities. Yet, at the same time, I had to face many challenges in my life. However, I was given the gift of wonderful tools that impacted my life in a very positive way, which led me through a journey of unique discovery and to a different level of thinking. I continue to study the gift of life and am being prepared to go around the world, sharing with others. The mental, spiritual, and ethical transformation I have been experiencing inspired me to write this book; before, I wouldn't have even thought about writing a book.

Now, I want to share this book with you, and I want you share it with others!

Be amazing!
Thank you,
Sandy Money

In my journey on this great planet Earth, I ask myself, "What is the purpose of me being here? What is the purpose of my life?" The answer is to serve God. I ask myself, "How can I serve God?" The answer came to me that to serve God, I must help as many people as possible, to lead them to find their purpose in life, and by doing that, they can live a happy and fulfilling life. We all have a gift within, but some of us forget how to bring them out. That is why we need someone to remind us, to give us some direction without judgment. It's why this book was born with the purpose to help you, especially for those who love to help others. If you enjoy helping others, this book is for you!

When I was going through an awful challenge in my life, I immersed myself into empowering books, CDs, and workshops. I went to many seminars to help me get through my challenges. Our world is hurting; it is time for us to come out and do something about it! It is time to stop being a spectator. To help many is to lead you to greatness! When I was going through my hardest times, I didn't want to go to a psychiatrist or psychologist, because I felt that my problem was not mental or in need of any medicinal drugs. It was more like temporary life challenges.

*OUR ATTITUDE
TELLS THE WORLD
WHAT WE EXPECT IN RETURN.*

I began my studies and questioning for knowledge about the meaning of true life in 1993.

After a painful divorce and with the tremendous responsibility of raising three children alone, I had lots of fears and doubts about life. I loved my children so much, I just had to put my children in God's hands and pray that I would do a good job raising them as productive human beings.

My desire to learn about self-empowerment, religion, spirituality, communication, goal setting, relationships, business, and finance, among many other topics, has led me on a unique journey of discovery. I've done many things in my life, owned many businesses, and one thing I have found very interesting is the self-discovery aspect of it all. I started educating myself more and more in that direction, and this book was born.

For over fifteen years, I have studied a wide variety of resources. I am nationally licensed and certified as a Master Neuro-Linguistic Programming Practitioner (NLP) and as a Time-Line Therapist and Train the Trainer through T. Harv Eaker. I have studied the works of Earl Nightingale, Anthony Robbins, Jim Rohn, Napoleon Hill, Wayne Dyer, Brian Tracy, Robert Kiyosaki, Blair Singer, Donald Trump, Al Thomas, Dr. John DeMartini, and God. They are my great master teachers and helped to contribute to my vast knowledge and wisdom that I am able to share with you.

*OUR ATTITUDE TOWARD LIFE
DETERMINES
LIFE'S ATTITUDE TOWARD US.*

I was born in South America (Peru) to an alcoholic father and a beautiful, loving mother. My father was musically talented, but he had a horrible alcohol addiction. He could not keep a job, let alone care about his children and wife. I used to see him intoxicated every day; I can't remember ever seeing him sober. The most horrifying moments were when I witnessed my mother being beaten by my dad. It hurt so much to watch that violence. Whenever I think about my mom in my later years, I can still feel and see the pain in her face from being abused. I can still remember those terrifying moments very vividly.

I remember my father loved to play the twelve-string guitar and harmonica, sing, and hang out at bars; those were his favorite things to do. He would be gone for days. My mother would go looking for him, wanting to be sure that he didn't get beaten by anyone; whenever he was intoxicated, he would go looking for a fight. From an early age, I was often left home alone and would stand by the window, looking out, crying, and hoping that my parents would come home soon. Sunup and sundown, and no Mom or Papa. I was so very scared and lonely!

I had three brothers: two older and one younger than I. I remember that many times we didn't even have food to eat. I never got to see the older ones since they lived with my grandparents, because of the situation and I don't remember the younger one very well. Thank God, my grandparents were very good to us, especially my mom's parents. My grandparents loved my mom, their only child. I remember my grandparents telling my mom to leave my dad, but my mom wouldn't listen to them.

I often asked myself, "Why is it that some women can't leave their abuser?" Watching my mom being abused mentally and physically was very traumatic for me. It took many years for me to overcome it, and the worst part was yet to come. Subconsciously, I married a man similar to my father. I couldn't believe it! The only difference was that I wasn't beaten physically like my mother, but I was emotionally torn apart, bit by bit. He was an alcoholic and lazy. Just think about what that is telling you. I paid a heavy price for not learning what I should have learned when I was subjected to those terrifying moments in my childhood.

POOR ATTITUDE =
POOR RESULTS
GREAT ATTITUDE =
GREAT RESULTS

My father used to drag my mother by her hair. She had long, beautiful hair, but it got so thin because of the repeated dragging. He would have chunks of her hair in his hands. I was so young and felt so helpless, because I couldn't help and defend my mom. The only thing I could do was cry and tell my father to stop hurting my mother. But he wouldn't listen to me; he just pushed me away. This episode happened many times. The most horrendous experience was when my father grabbed an axe and lifted it, ready to strike her. Thankfully, my older brother came out of nowhere and was able to grab the axe from my father's hands. I grabbed my father's legs, crying, screaming, and begging him, "Stop! Please stop! Don't hurt my mom, please!" By then, she was bleeding all over.

It was so painful to watch my father beat my mom. What kind of message is a child supposed to get from this experience? No child should have to go through such a negative and painful experience. Little children don't have control over adults. Parents can influence their children to be losers or winners. When a child grows up in an abusive home, it can damage that child's life and affect him or her for life. I know, because that happened to me. What I experienced in my childhood affected me emotionally in my adult life. And the pattern continues in my family. My older brother got married and has beautiful kids. But, like my father, he, too, plays the guitar, sings, and drinks very heavily—and beats his wife.

It is no wonder why so many people in the world are hurting, and many of them don't even know why! Why there is emotional pain and confusion? As a child, I watched my father, the man I loved, the one I looked up to, beat my mother, the woman who gave birth to me. Me, a tiny child, begged him to stop. He didn't care or think about my feelings, I know that. I carried these haunting memories all the way to my adulthood. When I had the opportunity to learn how to deal with and overcome those horrid childhood experiences, I first learned how to recognize the pain and find the solution, so I could find joy. It's very interesting that some women stay in the abusive relationship. Why? Because their hopes are bigger than their pain they experience from their abuser?

---

*YOUR ATTITUDE
TOWARD OTHERS
DETERMINES THEIR
ATTITUDE TOWARD YOU.*

I remember my grandmother telling my mom to move back home, but for some reason, she continued to stay with my father. She would never say anything bad about anyone, not even my dad. My mother was a real angel of God; now I know why God took her home. She was extremely sweet and loving. I know that God loved her very much, and that is why she's not here to be abused anymore. I understand now. Before, I couldn't understand why she left me. Growing up lonely, I used to be very envious of kids who had a mother. I used think, *Why do the other kids have a mom and not me? It's not fair!* I wanted to have a mom—even if I had to buy one. Well, I thought you could just buy a mom! Now that's funny, but it wasn't at the time.

My mother passed away when I was eleven or twelve years old. She died from childbirth, and that was the end of my world. She and I were home alone at the time. She was expecting a baby, and I guess it was time for the baby to be born. She didn't look well. I saw her in pain and asked, "Are you okay, Mama?" She said that she felt as though she was ready to have the baby, and the pain was getting worse by the minute. Seeing the pain in her face, I said to her, "I'm going to find help." I ran down the street, as fast as I could, hoping that I could find someone who could help us. I got to the neighbor's house and knocked desperately on the door. No one answered.

I went to the next neighbors' house and knocked on the door; no one answered there, either! I asked myself,

What am going to do now? I ran back home and told my mother that no one was home. She said, "Please go find the midwife who took care of me before." The midwife lived very far away, but I didn't care. I ran and ran, thinking I would never get there. Finally, I got there, I knocked on the door, and the midwife was not home. With no other choice, I went looking for another midwife. I ran so far; I don't even know how many miles. It was so far, but the pain that I saw in my mother's eyes gave me the strength to keep going. The worst part was that the other midwife was not home, either.

Disappointed and sad, I returned home, crying. When I got home, my mom was lying down in pain, her face so pale and cold sweat running down her forehead. I gave her the bad news, and she said, "It is okay." I felt helpless; I didn't know what to do. I was so afraid and frustrated. In those days, you could not call the ambulance. It was not like here in the United States, where you can just grab the phone and call for help. What a blessing it is that we have everything we need and want in this great country. After suffering through a long labor, the baby was born. It was a little boy! I looked at the baby in amazement. Oh wow! But the baby was not moving and was all blue. My mom said, "The baby is dead." She wrapped a little blanket around the baby. I was very sad, watching my little brother being born dead.

By then, my mom looked very weak. She told me she felt a little hungry and asked me if I can make soup. I had never made soup before, but I did my best and made chicken soup. I fed her with a spoon, because she could barely sit up. She only ate a couple of spoonfuls. Then, very softly, she told me how grateful she was to have a daughter like me.

THE DEEPEST CRAVINGS OF THE HUMAN BEING IS FOR RECOGNITION, SELF-ESTEEM, TO BE NEEDED, TO FEEL IMPORTANT, TO BE RECOGNIZED, AND TO BE APPRECIATED.

THAT INCLUDES OUR LOVED ONES AND EVERYONE ELSE WITH WHOM WE COME INTO CONTACT DURING OUR DAYS.

That was really sweet music to my ears. I remember being a good girl most of the time, as I had a special respect and love for my mom. I never mouthed-off to her. There was one thing, however. She used to tell me to brush my hair, and I didn't always obey, so when she brushed my hair, it would hurt. That left a bad memory for me, which I carried for a long time. I did not allow anyone to touch my hair until I was over twenty years old. If someone touched my hair without my permission, an angry feeling would overcome me, and I would want to scream out, "Don't touch my hair!" The first time someone cut my hair was when I was about twenty-two years old. I gave permission to the stylist to cut my hair, and little by little, I was freed of my fear. Can you see? Can you hear? Can you feel the childhood scars? It may be a small thing to the parents but such a big thing for a young mind and body.

Now, going back to the moment when I was with my mom, her words were music to my ears. During those painful moments, she had thought to give me words of assurance. It hurt so much watching her in such terrible pain. I felt so hopeless, unable to do anything that could make her pain go away. I was there but did not know what to do.

Finally, my father showed up, and as usual, he was drunk! He saw my mother dying. By then, she could barely talk. He lifted her head into his arms, started crying, and said to her, "Don't leave me, please!" At that moment, in her dying voice, she said to me, "There is someone at the door. The dogs are barking; let them in. They are coming for me." I went to open the door, and no one was there. Just us four, with the baby, and a few minutes later, my mother was gone forever. Oh my gosh! My whole world was shattered from that moment on.

After she died, our home was broken apart. Each of us kids was placed in a different place. My mother's parents took my younger brother, and my older brothers went with my dad's parents. I stayed with my dad. He tried to take care of me the best he could. I loved him because he was my father, and he never ever hurt me physically. I was his only daughter. Every time he came home, I ran to him to look in his pockets. I would always find something for me. One time, he said jokingly, "Next time, I am going to put a snake in my pocket, because your hands are always in my pockets," and he laughed!

TREAT EVERYONE WITH WHOM
YOU COME IN CONTACT AS
THE MOST IMPORTANT
PERSON ON EARTH;
START THIS HABIT AND
PRACTICE IT CONSISTENTLY.

Unfortunately, the alcohol addiction got the best of him. I think he got tired of dragging me back and forth with him. He decided to place me in a Catholic school, where I had to live there while I went to school. The plan was that I would become a nun, but I don't think that was my calling, because I was miserable. I felt as though I was in prison. My dad would come to see me every other weekend. They had very strict rules: get up at five o'clock in the morning, take a shower, make the bed, clean my room, go to mass, eat breakfast, and then class. There was no time to play!

Every time my dad came to see me, I would beg, "Please take me out of here!" I think he got tired of seeing me cry, so he took me out of the school. At that time, I did not understand what he was trying to do with me. I thought he was trying to abandon me, but now I look back and see he was just trying to do the right thing for me. That Catholic school could have been the best thing for me, but I was too young to understand. Then, my freedom was more important to me than becoming a nun. If I had stayed, by now I would be a Catholic nun, but at the same time, I would have missed out on my blessing of having three beautiful children. After he took me out of the school, I just hung around with him. I went where he went, which was of course, places where he could get drunk. While he got drunk, I ate my cookies and drank my soda pop. After he got super drunk, he would put me over his shoulders and carry me with him to find a place to sleep. I don't remember many other places besides the bars.

THERE ARE A FEW THINGS
MORE PITIFUL THAN THE
PERSON WHO WASTES HIS OR
HER LIFE,
RUNNING FROM ONE THING TO
ANOTHER,
FOREVER LOOKING FOR
THE GOLD AT THE END OF
THE RAINBOW AND NEVER
STAYING WITH ONE THING
LONG ENOUGH TO FIND IT.

Now, after many years, I still remember being on my dad's shoulders. Those were precious moments with him; I think it was the only time I felt connected to him. I don't remember where he dropped me off; he lost me. The addiction was so strong that he forgot whom he loved the most. It was no problem for me. I was just a kid who liked freedom. Now I could go anywhere I wanted; no one had control over me! You know when you are kid, it is a great feeling to be free. One week I stayed with my paternal grandparents, and the following week, I stayed with my momma's parents. Then I'd stay with my aunt, next some friends, and then I went to all different places. I'm thinking, *This is very fun!* I was enjoying my freedom, but that didn't last too long. Before long, I'm in the hands of the police. I don't really remember how I ended up in police custody, but I remember the officer asked me my age. I told him that I was twelve years old, and he asked me about my parents. I told him, "I don't have any parents." I explained to the officer that my mother was dead and I didn't know where my father was. I really didn't know where my father was. I was hoping that they might send someone to look for my father, but that didn't happen. The police officer took me to an orphanage and left me there.

That place was very different. There were a lot of kids at the beginning, and it was very exciting. I thought, *Wow! I have all these kids to play with, it's going to be so much fun!* But to my surprise, that place was like a prison.

There were too many rules, and I was in a strange place after I had enjoyed my freedom. I didn't like it at all. I wanted to get out or at least get in touch with someone from the outside world. This was a place for real orphans, and I tried to explain to the people who ran the orphanage that I had a family. They didn't believe me. They told me since the police brought me there, they were responsible for me. I just cried. I felt that I was in whole different world. It is not like here in the United States, where they investigate and try to find the kid's parents. They try get to the bottom of the problem as much as they can.

Now, I think back about the place, and it was not too bad. There were lots of rules, but they had to have lots of rules for that many kids. The place was all in order and had a very organized schedule. But I didn't like anybody to give me rules to follow, and that was what drove me crazy! Even now, I don't like being ordered around. Tell me once or twice what I have to do, and I will do more than expected, because I don't like to have someone boss me around. Even now, I don't have one, and I haven't had a boss for more than twenty years. I am very grateful for that! I'm my own boss, and that is a good feeling!

---

*HUMAN BEINGS SHOULD
NEVER BE SETTLED.
IT'S OKAY FOR ANIMALS,
BUT IT'S WRONG FOR
HUMAN BEINGS.
PEOPLE START TO DIE
WHEN THEY BECOME SETTLED.
WE NEED TO KEEP
THINGS STIRRED UP.*

Well, a couple of years later, I escaped from that orphanage. Oh boy! When they found out that I was gone, they called the police so they could find me and take me back there. I had to find an adult very quickly, before the police found me. Somehow, I found out that my cousin, with whom I used to be very close, was looking for me, too. I was so excited! I found her and told her everything that what was happening to me. She was older than I, of legal age, and she took me into her house. When the police found me, I was with my cousin. She told them that she was taking responsibility for me, so the police left me alone. Yes, I'm free again!

After that episode, I missed my mom so much! I decided to go find her, because in my mind, she was still alive somewhere. Even though I saw her being buried, I could not admit her death. So, I went on a journey to find my mom. I went to as many places as I could. Every time I saw a lady who looked like her, I wanted to ask her to be my mom; but I was too shy to ask. I just hung around, hoping she would take me with her. That never happened. I continued to wander from place to place, city to city. And when I got a little older, I went from country to country in search of my mother. I met a girl a couple of years older than I. Though I told her I was an orphan, I didn't tell her that I was looking for my mom. We became very good friends, her name was Marina. She took me into her home and introduced me to her mom, dad, brother, and sister. She and I became like sisters.

Her parents felt sorry for me, and when my friend asked them if I could live with them, they agreed I could stay. My friend and I worked together, we partied together; we had so much fun together. I became so close with her family that I said to her, "I wonder if your parents would like to adopt me?" She said, "I will ask my parents." She did ask them, and their response was yes, but they had to consult the other kids. They did, and the other kids were against it. They were afraid that they would have to split whatever inheritance their parents would leave. I didn't care about any material things; the only thing I wanted was to have a mom and dad. I even told the other kids, "I promise I won't take anything from your parents." They replied, "Yeah right! Legally you will have the right to have whatever my parents have." My friend, her parents, and I were very sad. They were very nice to me. I liked them so much, I used to call them Aunt and Uncle. Other times, I would call them Mom and Dad. I even looked a lot like my friend's father.

DON'T TRY TO RUN AWAY FROM
YOUR TROUBLES.
OVERCOME THEM.
PREVAIL RIGHT
WHERE YOU ARE.

I decided to continue looking for my mother, but by now, I was exhausted and very sad. I was also very upset and angry at my mother. In my loneliness, the only thing I did was cry, and in my cries, I asked my mother, "Why did you leave me? Don't you know that I need you? You left me when I needed you the most. Where are you? I'm calling you; why don't you answer me? Don't you understand that I miss you?" Oh my gosh! I cried and cried.

I would scream in my most agonizing voice, "Tell me, where I can find you? Mamaaaaa!" Before my mom's death, I had only experienced one death. My favorite aunt got sick and died, but two days later, she came back to life. I remember they were preparing the funeral already. Oh boy! Everybody was shaken up about her resurrection; that was a very amazing moment! A miracle! You see what I mean? At that time, I didn't understand death.

Now I do. I understand that my mom had no control over her death. I understand that no one has control over death. I give thanks to my spiritual teachers and the big book for teaching me and helping me to understand all about spirituality. Before, I didn't understand, which was why I searched for my mother even though she was dead. When I couldn't find my mother, my anger toward my father grew. I recalled what he did to her, her suffering before her death. I began to put everything together, and I realized her death was mostly caused by him and the beatings she took from him, even when she was pregnant.

I hadn't seen him for a long time, but my anger for him was still very strong, and I used to think, *I'm sure he's getting drunk somewhere.* The only person who never got physically hurt was me; everybody else took their beatings.

FREEDOM AND PERSONAL
LIBERTY
ARE THE MOST PRECIOUS
THINGS ON EARTH,
TO GET TO AMERICA DESPITE
MOUNTAINOUS PROBLEMS
AND MILES TO FIND
THEMSELVES FREE FOR THE
FIRST TIME IN THEIR LIVES

It is very sad that we are born into this world with free will, and many people choose destructive behavior. Most of them hurt not only themselves but their loved ones as well. They choose to take part in alcohol, legal drugs/illegal drugs, sex, or eating addictions. All addictions are destructive and affects everyone around the person with the problem. The person with an addictive behavior chooses a slow death. An individual with an addiction says it's his problem and no one else's, but the truth is that it affects everyone else around him. The person with an addiction exudes very negative energy. You can be strong and try to resist, but if you continue to stay with that person, he will, little by little, suck your energy dry! The most horrifying experience I had was watching my mother being tortured by my father; that was hard to understand. Watching him almost kill my mom can really mess up one's mind, especially when you are very young. I used to wonder, *Is that love? Is love supposed to be painful?* When you are just a kid, it is hard to understand love versus violence.

Well, I continued looking for my mother; I missed her so much. I wanted my family life back so very badly! "Oh my God!" I said to myself. "I have no Mom to love me or to care for me." I felt that family life was over for me. Soon I became homeless. I slept anywhere; sometimes the cement floor was the mattress and the newspaper was my sheet. I went many days without eating. I felt so lonely! I didn't know where I belonged, and I wanted someone to adopt me so badly. I longed for a mom and dad, but I was not lucky enough to have them, so I grew up alone and emotionally lost.

When I was homeless, it never occurred to me to take any drugs, beg for money, or shoplift, and no one taught me right from wrong. Maybe my mom taught me, but I couldn't remember much; I know I didn't learn these things from my father. He was a very dishonest man who would lie, cheat, and steal at every opportunity that came to him. For me, I was the opposite. Honesty and integrity were very important, and earning a person's trust was very crucial to me from a very young age.

Well, by now I am seventeen years old, a little bit older and more mature after being homeless. I found a job at a community bank, I worked there for a while and I was able to save some money. I started to travel outside of Peru in search for my mother. I went to Brazil, Ecuador, Bolivia, Argentina, Columbia, and Venezuela. In every country, I found a job, so I was never homeless again. I found Venezuela to be a very interesting country, and I decided to stay there for a little while. I liked it so much that I decided to stay much longer and to settle down. I was eighteen years old. As time went by, I became very active in politics. I had a job and was making good money now, which was a great feeling. Then, I decided to become an actress. I went to school to study theater and acting. I wanted to be sure that I would be studying at the best acting school, so I did my research. I found the best school, which was the Academy of Arts Juana the Sojo.

I had the best teacher, Mr. Porferio Rodriguez. Soon, I was introduced to the TV industry and photo novels (magazine). I was enjoying life and had a great future waiting for me. I had lots of friends, and exciting things were happening for me. But, at age twenty-two, I still felt an emptiness inside of me.

IN AMERICA, YOU CAN GET ANYTHING YOU WANT. THE TROUBLE IS,
MANY AMERICANS DON'T KNOW WHAT THEY WANT.

I lived in Venezuela for seven years, the longest I had ever stayed in one place. Then, with my God's blessing, I found the way to come to the United States of America, to the country of freedom. I had wanted to come to the United States since I was very young. When I shared my dreams and desires to come to the United States, people would laugh at me and say I was crazy. They would tell me, "You will never be able to get a visa." So many people try to get a visa, but they would be declined all the time. Those people told me to forget my dreams, that I would never be able to go to the United States. I didn't want to give in to their opinion, so I kept hoping that someday I would go to the United States. I had it engraved on my heart.

I remember when I was very young and living in Peru, John F. Kennedy was president of the United States. The president of Peru was a dictator, he hated President Kennedy so much. I was very young and didn't understand why. No U.S. products were allowed in Peru, because the dictator had a lot of anger toward the United States. This was nonsense, because the United States is a very powerful country, and other countries are very jealous because they feel powerless over the United States. Think about it. If the United States were a weak country, we would be in the dragon's mouth. This country didn't become powerful overnight; it took a long time, and much blood was shed. As far as I know, this country doesn't use its power to try to take over helpless countries. Instead, it acts as a protector, like a big brother. God has blessed this country with great things, and God is watching over us. For me, this is the Promised Land. I believe it is not an accident that I am here and have become a part of this great country, for which I am very grateful.

WE TALKED ABOUT FREEDOM AND ABOUT HOW DEAR IT IS TO THOSE WHO NEVER HAD IT, WHILE MOST AMERICANS TAKE IT FOR GRANTED AND NEVER EVEN THINK ABOUT IT.

Somebody once manufactured a T-shirt with a beautiful American flag on it. Whoever manufactured the T-shirts had a lot of guts, because in those days, anybody showing support for the United States would be put in jail. Not young kids, of course, so I took advantage of my age and bought the T-shirts. I wore one almost every day. I was so proud and dreamed that someday I would go to the United States of America! I thank God every day for giving me the opportunity to journey to the United States and be a part of this beautiful country, the land of freedom, which I love with all my heart. I thank the American people for their willingness to share their country with me.

Before I came here, I lived in Venezuela. Life was great, and I seemed to have a great future with much success. Many doors were opening for me, especially when I started acting school. I received an offer to do some parts in one of the soap operas that was going to be featured on TV. I accepted the offer, and the next offer was to do a photo novel for a weekly soap opera magazine. Also, working with a company that promoted musical shows, I got the opportunity to meet Liza Minnelli when she was just starting in the show business. I also met Julio Iglesias and Ricky Martin when he was with the Puerto Rican group Menudo. I met the famous Venezuelan singer Jose Luis Rodriguez.

Despite my success, deep in my heart was still the desire to come to the United States. One day I had enough courage and went to the U.S. Embassy to find out what was required to get a visa. The people who worked there were very nice. I asked someone about getting a visa, one said, "I will be more than happy to give you all the information that you need." I thought, *Whoa, they are very nice!* Not at all how the other people told me it would be; but I had gone there with a positive attitude. To get a visa, one was required to have so much money in the bank, a great work record, proof of work, a clean criminal record, medical records, and one had to have some shots before entering the United States. They would have to verify one's information to make sure everything was okay. I said, "Thank you very much." I went home. Thank God I had everything they needed from me. Can you imagine if everyone followed the requirements? We would be in good shape. The requirements, in my opinion, are just protecting the people from here. To enter the United States should be a privilege, and when we are here, we must treat it with respect. I gathered all my papers, went back to the embassy, and turned in everything required. After one of the workers reviewed my application, she said, "Everything looks good. Come back in two weeks."

FOR MANY PEOPLE, THE SECRET OF HAPPINESS IS FREEDOM, AND THE SECRET OF FREEDOM IS COURAGE

Now I just had to wait two weeks; it felt like two months! After two weeks, I went back to the embassy, and there was my ticket to freedom: my passport was beautifully stamped with a visa that granted me permission to enter the United States of America. Oh my gosh! I was jumping for joy when she said to me, "Congratulations, you're being granted a visa to enter the United States." When I went back to the embassy, I didn't know what to expect. All the negative little voices from the people were going through my mind: "You will never be able get an American visa. It's very hard, and they will laugh at you." "There is no way you can get a visa!" People used to say, "Forget your stupid, crazy dreams." They even took me to a movie that was supposed to be about American life. I don't remember the movie's title, but the movie was very gross. It was all about prostitution, drug addicts, homelessness, the gross food industry, and many other things. It sure does shake your mind, but in spite of all that, I was determined to come here. When she gave me my passport, I was so happy I didn't know whether to hug her or kiss her I looked at the stamp in my passport over and over.

I ran back home. No one would believe me. They thought I was losing my mind. So I put the visa in their faces. After they saw it, they finally believed me and now they wanted to know how I did it. If I had listened to all the negative advice that people gave me, I would have missed out on my opportunity to be here. Many try to get a visa but are denied. I was blessed. I had a great desire and faith. I knew that I was a good person, always looking for ways in which I could become successful in life. I was also willing to help others. I love people! They are a gift from God (especially the children).

Now, I just had to catch my plane. I flew in on one of the beautiful, jumbo, German planes right before they stopped flying to the United States. I landed at LA International Airport, of course, so I could be close to Hollywood, since one of my goals was to continue my acting career. When I got off the plane, I was kind of confused. Everywhere I turned, they spoke Spanish. I asked a guy at the airport, "Sir, is this the United States of America?" The man said, "Sí, señorita." Then he asked me, "Why? Are you going to New York?" "Oh no," I replied. "I just wanted to make sure." He said, "Okay, señorita!" I went to get my luggage and catch the taxicab to find a hotel. I had to stay in a hotel, because I didn't know anyone. I ended up in North Hollywood, where there was a hotel attached to the YMCA.

THE BEST DEFINITION OF SUCCESS IS THIS: SUCCESS IS THE PROGRESSIVE REALIZATION OF A WORTHY GOAL, AS LONG AS WE'RE WORKING TOWARD SOMETHING. THAT'S WHEN A HUMAN BEING IS AT HIS OR HER BEST.

I had been in LA for three months when I began to wonder how I was going to learn English, since most people seemed to speak Spanish. Oh, and I almost got killed there in Los Angeles. So I decided to visit Las Vegas. I knew Las Vegas from the movies. Oh my goodness. I found Las Vegas to be so beautiful and different. *Oh great! The people here speak English,* I thought, so I made Las Vegas my home and have been here since 1981. My English was not very good, and I decided that I was not going to be a non-English-speaking immigrant. I was very determined to learn how to speak English, so everything I did was in English. I read the newspaper, watched TV in English, and enrolled in a community college to take an English as a second language class. I had taken an English class before coming to the United States, but it's not the same thing. "I love this great country, so I must speak English if I want to be part of it," I told myself. "I will speak English, and there is no other option." That was the commitment I made to myself.

We have so many opportunities here to take advantage of and do something with. Or, you can choose to live your life, complaining about it or the government. You don't know the horrible things that people have to go through just to be able to survive in some countries. People who complain about this country have no idea what they are talking about. I want them to go and try to live in another country—like somewhere in South America, Central America, Asia, or the Middle East—but be sure not to take U.S. dollars with you. Then, try to have the same or better lifestyle than you had here. See how you like it! I strongly agree with John F. Kennedy, when he stated, "Don't ask what your country can do for you, ask what you can do for your country." Does the message mean anything to you? What I hear from most people is the entitlement syndrome. Where I came from there are no such things such as food stamps, and other benefits.

---

*IT'S ABOUT 90 PERCENT
MENTAL ATTITUDE.
OUR MENTAL ATTITUDE CAN
MAKE ALL THE DIFFERENCE
BETWEEN WINNING
AND LOSING.*

Here, the U.S. government is very generous, and you never end up in the street unless you choose to. When I was just a kid, I heard a speech by a U.S. president JF. Kennedy. I was very young and didn't understand politics. I wonder if people forgot about that speech. In this country, the government wants people to become entrepreneurs. You even get tax credits if you build a business. The government gives you choices to pay your taxes before or after the year ends. If you live paycheck to paycheck, you pay your tax every time you get paid. But if you are an entrepreneur, you pay your tax at the end of the year, after you write off all of your expenses. What a great deal! Maybe if more people understood this system, there wouldn't be so many poor people, and they wouldn't have to make movies like *Robin Hood*, where he robs the rich to give to the poor instead of teaching the people how to fish so they have food for life! The United States is not a communist country. In communist countries, people have no freedom; they don't have freedom to do whatever they want! The government dictates to them the lifestyle they should have, and people have no public opinion about anything; they are like robots. The government thinks people are stupid and can't choose their own future.

One day I was talking to a Russian man about his family. He looked very, very sad. I asked him, "Are you okay?" He answered in a very sad voice, "You know, Sandy, I really miss my mom. She's getting old, and I would like for her to be here with me. I know she would like that, too, but she's so afraid." I asked him, "Why?" He said, "If she comes to United States to live with me, she will lose all of her benefits, and she's afraid about that." When Russia was a communist country, the government controlled everything. They were given an allowance and a little place to live. Wow! That's why I said never mind a four- or six-bedroom home or nice convertible cars to drive and a vacation in Hawaii or Disney World! When a person's freedom has been taken away, life becomes nothing!

Don't let anyone decide your freedom for you!

You might have a desire to be rich and successful, but you think you can't. You may ask why. The answer is your freedom has been taken away! Your freedom, your God-given freedom! I'm so grateful that I live in the United States, where we have freedom to do whatever we want, within the law, and become whomever we want to be. Let freedom make sounds of joy! I thank God every day for my freedom, and I understand freedom is not really free. Someone had to sacrifice his or her life for our freedom, and we must not forget that!

JOY AND SATISFACTION COME TO US FROM SERVING OTHERS, AND THERE ARE MILLIONS OF WAYS OF DOING THAT, AND CHANCES ARE YOU WILL BE RICHLY REWARDED.

We can be rich if we choose to or be poor; the choice is ours, not the government's. By being poor, you're only living half of your greatness, but if that is comfortable for you, it is okay! The sky is the limit for those who want to be successful! I promised myself to be a productive human being and not a liability to this great country. I want to give back my love and appreciation for this country, because what this country gave me helped me become who I am today.

A couple of years after I got here, I decided to join the military. I went to a recruiting center, located at Sahara Avenue and Las Vegas Boulevard, that had stations for the marines, air force, and the army. The air force was my first choice, but my height was not in my favor; I was only 5'1" tall; their height requirement was a few inches taller. They advised me to go to the army. I went to the army, and they were so glad to see me. But I ran into another problem: my English was not good enough for them. They were right; my English was very broken. I thought, *Oh no! There goes my chance to serve this country!* They were very nice about it and told me to come back after I learned to read and write English clearly. I was very disappointed, but I couldn't do anything about it at the time.

So I continued learning English. I had other plans and goals, such as getting my citizenship. I learned if I got my citizenship, I would be able to vote. That was very exciting to me—the privilege to vote! To obtain citizenship, I had to wait for five years, so I waited anxiously for five years to become American citizen. When you are waiting for something very important, it feels like you're waiting forever! After waiting for four years, I submitted my petition. I had to do it a year early, because it takes a whole year to get approved or denied. While I waited, I studied U.S. history and learned the Pledge of Allegiance. One part in a history lesson got my attention: the Declaration of Independence, I don't know if some people would notice what this means. The declaration says independence—for us to be independent from the government—it isn't a declaration of dependence, and this country was founded under God. Let us not forget how the government was created for the people by the people. After waiting for five years, I became a U.S. citizen. What a joy! I thank God that my petition was approved without any problem.

*SINCE NO TWO PEOPLE ARE
EXACTLY ALIKE,
IT STANDS THAT NO TWO OF US
WILL HAVE EXACTLY
THE SAME GOALS;
AT SAME TIME, NO ONE
GETS RICH WITHOUT
ENRICHING OTHERS.*

When I came here, my plan was to continue my acting career, but God had other plans for me. I got married to a great professional golfer. He was a very good-looking man known as "Mr. 58," a Guinness World Record holder. Soon after, I became a mother, and the rest is history. I have three beautiful children, one girl and two boys: Mary, Bryan, and Michael. My husband was a great golfer, but his alcohol addiction was greater. I was not aware of the addiction. I had an alcoholic father, and I didn't even know! The addiction was not the only problem. The mental abuse of me and our kids was a horrible experience. I stayed married for eleven years. Where I came from, divorce was unheard of. I never saw people get married, divorced, married, and divorced. Here, men change wives like changing shirts. Here, people get divorced for little things. In my opinion, most divorces stem from selfishness; the individuals only think about themselves, not about the other person or their children. The children, the silent victims, pay the heavy price for the adults' selfish decisions. I think divorce should be the last resort; the only time divorce should be the answer is if the other partner is abusive and refuses to get help.

My case was very different, as I had no other choice. I had to protect my children from physical and emotional abuse. I was 100 percent responsible for my children's safety, so I had to choose between my children and him. It was not an easy decision to make, because I really loved him, and I was afraid to be alone and raise the three children without a father. I had to gather some strength and divorce him before I killed myself. Before my divorce, I became very suicidal. I was trying to find a way out, and at the time, I didn't know how. I was so desperate and lost, I didn't want be alive anymore. At the same time, I didn't want leave my kids without a mother. I was very overweight, almost 200 pounds and only 5'1". Can you imagine what I looked like? Food was my best friend, since I had no other friends and didn't want to see anybody.

POWER PRINCIPAL

WRITE DOWN EVERYTHING YOU CAN THINK OF THAT YOU WOULD REALLY LIKE TO SEE COME ABOUT IN YOUR LIFE, AND WORK TO ACHIEVE THEM ONE BY ONE.

Before I got married, I was very happy, beautiful, and courageous. That part of me was all gone after a few years of marriage. I became nothing, I forgot who I really was, I lost my identity. Now I can say that all those feelings were because I was focusing on the other person's problem. I gave away my freedom, or I shall say, I allowed him to take charge over my feelings. I became so focused on my husband's addiction; I used to think that I could change him. Now I know that there is no way you can change another human being's behavior. At that time, I was very unwise to try to change someone's behavior. Later, I realized that we have no power to change other person's attitude. But we have the power to change *our* behavior or attitude. That time in my life was so dark I felt like I was neck-deep in a hole and couldn't find my way out. So I decided that I didn't want to live anymore, and the only way out for me was to commit suicide.

I felt like the problems were suffocating me. I thought about divorce many times, but at same time, I was very weak and frightened by the thought of raising three children alone. I used to ask myself, "How am I going to do it, how am I going to be a mother and father to the children? Can I do good job raising the kids alone?" I don't know why I was asking myself all of those questions, because he was seldom home anyway. The way I learned how to raise children was by reading books, going to child development workshops, and by watching other people. I didn't know how to raise kids. I had no role model to follow on how to be a parent, and the fear of being alone was very daunting to me at the time.

I don't know why I was afraid of raising them alone, because the children's father was always away on a golf or bar trip. We hardly ever saw him, and when he came home, he was always drunk. Every time he came home drunk, he looked so mean there were times I used to hide my kids in the closet so he wouldn't mess with them. Whenever he got the kids, he pretended he was playing with them, but it was in a mean way. He would tickle them until they couldn't breathe. They would start to turn blue and choke. Meanwhile, he would be laughing, while the children were screaming and crying. There were other times he would throw one of them against the wall or the ceiling, and when they cried, he'd yell at them, "Stop crying! Don't be stupid! Be tough, chicken shit!" He would call them many other names that I don't want to mention in this book. After picking on the kids and me, he would pass out.

I HOPE YOU WILL PRACTICE THE MESSAGE IN THIS BOOK. ONE THING YOU CAN BE SURE OF, YOU WILL BECOME WHAT YOU THINK ABOUT MOST OF THE TIME.

I tried to stop him from hurting the kids, but he was very strong, and he would make fun of me, saying, "What are you going to do about it? Ha hah! You can't do anything. You're not strong like me, and these little wimps can't do anything either, because I'm strong!" By now, every one of us would be crying, and in that moment, I did feel helpless. He was big and strong, and my heart hurt so much for my little ones. Now I know that fear is crippling, and my fears kept me crippled. I didn't divorce sooner, letting the time pass for so long, because of that crippling fear that makes victims of many of us. Among my broken thoughts was the idea that if I ended my life, I wouldn't have to go through this experience anymore. So I started planning how to end my life, as well as that of my kids.

I grew up as an orphan, so I knew I didn't want to leave my kids without a mother. Because I experienced that situation firsthand, I knew that growing up without a mother is very painful. There are not enough words to describe the life of being an orphan. I loved my kids so much I didn't want them to suffer anymore, and I didn't want to place them in a foster home, either. Who knows what might happen to them, what kind of people they would be with. You hear of horrible things happening in foster homes. All those thoughts were going through my suicidal mind. One day I was trying to figure how to end my life with my children. I needed a very good plan, and it had to be very affective; no one could survive. That day, as

I tried to figure out how to end our lives, I was pacing back and forth in my living room. Suddenly a newsflash came on the television, stating that a lady with two children was under arrest, because she drowned her two little boys by driving a car into a lake. They mentioned she intended to be drowned with the kids, but at the last minute, she changed her mind and was able to get out. Unfortunately, she couldn't save the two boys. I was so shocked, and I said to myself, "Oh my gosh, that lady was supposed to be me!" Instead, it was her. I felt a trembling all over my body. I cried for her and the two boys. A question lingered in my mind. *What kind of pain had she experienced for her to do what she did?* I felt so much compassion for her and the two little boys.

MANY HUMAN BEINGS WOULD GIVE ANYTHING THEY HAVE TO ENJOY THE FREEDOM AND PERSONAL LIBERTY
YOU AND I TAKE FOR GRANTED; YOU HAVE THE RIGHT TO CHOOSE YOUR WORK AND GOALS, TO ENJOY THE BOUNTIFUL STANDARD OF LIVING, TO KNOW THE PEACE AND PRIVACY OF OUR HOMES, AND TO HAVE LAWS THAT PROTECT THE CITIZEN RATHER THAN PERSECUTE THEM.

This was a message from God to me; he was trying to show me something that I had to see through someone else before I followed through with my plans of suicide. I understood it to be a wake-up call for me. I said, "Okay, cancel the suicidal thought." Now, I needed to find a way out without committing suicide and to get out of the relationship. As I said before, I was full of fear and doubt. I now know how adversity can engulf us when we allow it to make us to think that there is no other way. In my situation, the answer for me, at the time, was to end precious lives. In reality, ending precious lives was not the answer. I now realize life is a gift from above. I also realize that by taking our lives, we are being ungrateful. When I understood that life was given to us as a gift from God, I changed the way I prayed. I used to pray to die, and now I pray to live. I also understood that God was always with me, even in my darkest times. I didn't realize until that one day in my living room—pacing back and forth, thinking about what to do. I decided to lie on the couch. I had so many questions. I had a lot of fear and despair. But, at that moment, I heard a voice saying, "Get out of the hole! Shake yourself off. You are not here to fail; you are here to win!" After hearing that voice, I looked around, but no one was there. For a moment, I thought I was going crazy, but at the same time, I felt a sense of peace running through my body. I felt as though I was waking up from a deep sleep.

Now I realize that God knows our pains and struggles. He never abandons us; we abandon ourselves—and him. Immediately I called my friend, Julie, my only friend at the time and the only one that I kept in touch with. I told her what happened to me, and she said, "Sandy, you are like an angel, the most caring and loving person who has been through so much pain, and you were able to endure it all. I always knew that God loves you very much." Those were very sweet words, and I told her, "I want to go back to church and do whatever I need to do to become a part of God's plan." I had stopped going to church a long time before, because I didn't want to see or talk to anybody except one person—my friend, Julie, my beautiful and loyal friend. She didn't care how I behaved or what I looked like; she loved me for who I was. I told Julie that I wanted to know more about God. By now, I realized that my creator was always there for me, especially in my darkest times. I was so busy thinking about myself that I had forgotten about my creator.

THE PERSON WITHOUT A
PURPOSE IS LIKE A SHIP
WITHOUT A MAP,
IT HAS NO FINAL DESTINATION.

I got divorced, and my journey to transform myself began. I began searching for ways to become a better person. I was aware there were things that I needed to change, and I had a strong desire to make those changes. I made an inventory of the areas that needed a change. I started reading many books in the area of human behavior, I began listening to many self-help CDs, and I went to self-improvement seminars. With those tools, I learned how to overcome many of my challenges. I was able to gather many tools and much information and then apply them to help me get through my adversity. I know that God made those tools available for me, because he knew that I needed to change. I'm very grateful to God. He was always there for me. I was blind and couldn't see the beauty that he blessed me with! I was deaf; I didn't hear his whispering, telling me he loved me and I was not alone! After the divorce was final, I felt a relief, although at the same time, I thought, *From now on, I will be the father and the mother.* I never thought I would be raising three children alone, and that was very scary, but I had no other choice. Mary was ten years old, Bryan eight years old, and Michael six years old. It was very tough. I had to work ten hours a day, six days a week, so I could put food on the table and have a roof over our heads, and have clothes to wear.

It was especially difficult when they were going into their teenage years. I was getting tired of not getting any financial help from their father, so I asked him for financial help. He said to me, "If you can't handle them, why don't you give them up for adoption?" That answer was very cruel to me; I couldn't believe what I was hearing. He knew that I loved my children so much I could never give them away. I was willing to do anything before I giving them up. I tried to open a child support case, but that didn't work. Because he refused to work, I couldn't get any money from him. He had no problem not working, because he lived off his dad. He told me, "You will never get money from me." Even the judge apologized, saying, "I am so sorry. I am trying to enforce the ruling, but he doesn't want to cooperate. Unfortunately, I can't force him to work, because it is the human's right."

We went back and forth in court. Then, he said he was getting tired of being back and forth in court, so he wanted to give up his parental rights. That way, he didn't have to pay child support. I told him, "You will never be able to see the kids!" He said, "That is okay! They will be coming and looking for me when they grow up." Oh my! I was shocked and appalled to hear that remark. I wondered how in the world I had picked this man to be the father of my children.

THE HUMAN MIND IS ONE
THING THAT *SEPARATES*
US FROM THE REST OF THE
CREATURES ON EARTH;
EVERYTHING THAT MEANS
ANYTHING TO US
COMES TO US THROUGH
OUR MINDS.

As the kids got older, becoming teenagers, Bryan was becoming uncontrollable. I had no one to turn to for help except his father. One day I asked him for help with Bryan. "Would you please keep Bryan with you for a little while? He's being very mean to his little brother and sister." He said yes, and our house was a little more peaceful. But not for long. A couple of weeks later, Bryan showed up at my work, drunk and crying. He said, "Mom, I am very sorry for what I've done! I've been drinking!" I was absolutely shocked, and I asked him, "How did you get alcohol?" He answered, "My dad has been buying it for me." Now, he's only twelve years old, and his father was buying my child hard liquor, Wild Turkey to be exact! I was crying, asking myself how or who I could trust to take care of my kids. It was like a nightmare. I was really freaking out at what I saw and heard from my twelve-year-old son. Oh my God. My children's father is supposed to be helping me raise a healthy kid and not destroying him. I hated him so much. I used to wish that I were a man, so I could go and beat him up for all the pain and suffering he put us through.

I was reading the Bible one day and came upon a passage that said to never take your own revenge but leave room for wrath of God, for it is written, "Vengeance is mine" (Romans 12:19). That really was powerful message for me. I learned to have more faith in God, and he would take care of the rest. As the time went by, the children's father developed all kinds of illnesses, such as high blood pressure, and liver, heart, and kidney ailments. He got his wish to never work again and had to go on disability. And, despite all those ailments, he still drinks! Later, I found out that he provided my other children with alcohol, and I couldn't believe that happened. How can it be possible their own father is leading them in the wrong path, while I am doing the best of my ability to raise them right? I tried to stop the kids from going to see him, but they would get angry with me and tell me, "You can't stop us from going to see our dad!" I answered, "I don't want to stop you from seeing your father. I just want to prevent you kids from the bad influence of addiction." He used to live very close to us, so when they wanted to see him, I would tell them to be careful, and they would walk to see him almost every day.

It is amazing to see the innocent and pure love children have for their parents, regardless of what they went through or how much pain they may have suffered. Children can be so forgiving. Many adults take this love for granted. Only children can have such a love that they don't hold any hate or anger toward him. I am very happy for the way my children are. My kids are over twenty years old and are very successful.

IF YOU WANT TO DEVELOP THE MUSCLES OF YOUR BODY, ENGAGE IN DAILY EXERCISE. A MIND IS DEVELOPED IN THE SAME WAY: WHERE YOUR MIND FOCUSES, THAT IS WHERE YOUR ENERGY IS ALSO.

> I am a strong believer that there is no joy without pain or pain without joy.

My children are very close to their father, and I am friends with him as well. I believe if I want to change and grow emotionally, mentally, and spiritually, I must forgive those who hurt me so that I can grow and move forward. The hatred, anger, and grudge-holding against those who hurt us are not productive to our success. If you want to win, you must learn to forgive for your own good. It's worth it!

>God gave us the freedom to choose<

LEARN TO ENJOY EVERY
MINUTE OF YOUR LIFE.
BE HAPPY NOW.
DON'T WAIT FOR SOMEONE
OR SOMETHING OUTSIDE
OF YOURSELF TO MAKE
YOU HAPPY; HAPPINESS
IS AN INSIDE JOB.

I guess I had more lessons to learn about relationships. A few years later, I met a guy, dated him for three years, and then we decided to get married. I thought I knew him well enough, but that was not the case. On our honeymoon, we took a trip to California. We took my car, because my car was paid off and nicer. It was only a few years old, so I trusted him with my car. I thought he was good driver, but was I wrong. We were on the California roads, headed to our destination, but we never got there. He ran a red light and another car hit us on the right passenger side, where I was sitting. The next thing I knew, I was waking up at the hospital; it was a miracle that I was not killed. He was fine, thank God. Unfortunately, I was a mess. I had no fractures, but it felt as if my internal organs had shifted from my right side to the left! When I checked out of the hospital, I saw my totaled car. I had to call the insurance and get a rental car to drive back to Las Vegas. Now, I didn't have a car to get to work or to take my kids to school. He was still living in his apartment. A month later, he moved in into my house and forced me to buy a new car, which I did. What was more interesting was that he didn't even volunteer to help with the payments. His credit was very bad, so he couldn't qualify to buy a car.

Thank God, I had no physical injuries, only emotional ones. But because of the emotional injuries, it took a whole year before I was able to get myself all together again. Right after we got back to Las Vegas, he started complaining about me, saying that I was acting strange, and he didn't feel that I wanted him! I couldn't understand what he was talking about. I was trying to be strong and ignoring my emotional pain; I didn't want him to see me going through the pain. I didn't want him to worry about me. Later, I explained to him what I was feeling, but that didn't do any good. He kept complaining, saying he didn't feel love from me. I told him, "I can't force you to believe me if you choose not to." He would complain almost every day about simple things. He became very jealous and controlling.

Suddenly, after two months of being married and living at my house, he decided to move out. When he moved out, I felt very sad and abandoned. I felt so much pain in my heart. I decided to seek an attorney to find out if I could annul the marriage since I was married only three months. The attorney stated that the procedure would be the same as a divorce. I chose not follow through with it at the moment. The attorney suggested I file a lawsuit for the pain and suffering that he created for me. I must say the idea sounded good, but I remembered the biblical passage about never taking your own revenge and leaving room for the wrath of God: "Vengeance is mine" (Romans 12:19). I just left it in God's hands, and thank goodness, I knew how to make the choice this time. I had the choice of falling on my face and dying, or standing up straight and move forward. So I chose to stand up straight, move forward, and when he was ready to walk out, I told him, "If you walk out through that door, don't you ever come back." He left and never came back.

A year later, I got divorced and that was the end of that learning experience. And now we are friends! A few years later, I found out that he had type II diabetes and has to take shots every day. On top of that, he has a girlfriend who is very abusive.

YOU WILL HEAR PEOPLE SAY
MONEY WON'T BUY HAPPINESS.
MONEY HAS BROUGHT A
LOT MORE HAPPINESS THAN
POVERTY HAS.
MONEY IS A WARM HOME AND
HEALTHY CHILDREN;
IT IS BIRTHDAY PRESENTS AND
A COLLEGE EDUCATION;
TO HELP OLDER PEOPLE
AND THE LESS FORTUNATE.

>You reap what you sow!<

It is very important to plant good seeds in good soil and to give good care. Be sure to water the seeds and keep away the birds and the bugs, so you can harvest healthy crops.

The universe gives us back what we send out!

Remember, we are all human, and as humans, we are all connected, regardless of who we are, color, shape, rich, or poor.

THE AMOUNT OF
MONEY WE RECEIVE
WILL ALWAYS BE
THE DIRECT RATIO
OF THE DEMAND FOR
WHAT WE DO.

To my surprise, there was another lesson on relationships in store for me. A couple of years later, I had the pleasure of meeting another gentleman. I knew him as a friend for a year. Later, he asked me to be his girlfriend; he seemed very nice, so I accepted. Well, by now you might be asking, "Didn't you learn your lesson?" I reply, "I believe in love, okay!" A few months later, he asked me to marry him, but I didn't take it too seriously. He asked again a bit later, and I still didn't take it too seriously. He wouldn't give up and asked me a third time. This time I accepted. I figured he was very serious, which is why I took it seriously. Before we got married, I prayed and asked God if I was doing the right thing by marrying him. The feeling I got was very strange, like saying,"You are on your own." I didn't understand what that meant, so I ignored the message. I thought, *What could be wrong with him? He seems so nice.* So I decided to marry him anyway. We got married in his living room, with two witnesses and my two kids. He didn't want anybody else to know that we were getting married. That was strange, but I was hypnotized by his charm.

He was almost perfect, every woman's dream. I thought he fell from heaven. One of my sons even said, "Mom, he is next to Jesus." My kids really liked him, especially my younger boy, who was fifteen years old at the time and called my new husband, "Dad". Lo and behold, there was a surprise in store for me. Thirty days later, he told me that he made a mistake by marrying me. He did not love me, and he wanted out. He then proceeded to tell me that he had a porno and sex addiction. I couldn't believe what I heard. I felt as though a bucket full of ice water had been poured over my head! For a moment, I was paralyzed and confused.

I thought I was dreaming, but unfortunately, it was real. Well, now I had a big decision to make: I could feel like a victim, sorry for myself, or I could stand up strong and face my challenge. I knew that I had a choice, thank God! I had my power tools with me now! I told him, "I know that you want me out, but I'm not going anywhere!" He hugged me, saying, "I don't want you to leave me! You're right, it's not about you! *I* have the problem." I replied, "Whatever problem you may have you own, and you must learn how to deal with it. If you allow me to help you, I will and do whatever I can to help you. But I will not take your blame!"

It was very peaceful for few months. Then, he asked me if it was okay for him to have another wife. At this time, I just played his game. I told him, "Sure, you can have as many wives as you want, if you can afford it." Soon, he kicked out my daughter and started picking on my younger son. My three children and I are very close, and before we got married I told him, "My kids are my world, and they go wherever I go." He said, "That is great. Even if you had 100 kids, I would still want to marry you." In the beginning, he was extremely nice to my kids, but it didn't last for long.

―――――――――――――――

NOW ASK YOURSELF, HOW MUCH DO YOU WANT? HOW MUCH MONEY DO YOU NEED TO LIVE IN THE WAY YOU WANT TO LIVE?

―――――――――――――――

One day we were just conversing about things. He paused for a moment and then proceeded to tell me that, in his mind, he undresses every woman he sees and wants to take them to bed. Afterward, he said to me, "You are in my way, stopping me from being able to continue doing what I enjoyed when I was single." My view of this man's behavior was that he was facing a battle between good and evil. He had two personalities: one part of him was screaming to be loved and wanted to be a good husband and father. Oh, I almost forgot to mention that he was married twice before me and had two kids, one with each woman. How typical! The other part of him wanted to do all sorts of crazy stuff. Every thirty days, he would transform into that mean person, who was very loud, used very bad words, and broke things. It was awful! After he was done with his craziness, he would apologize to us, crying, "I am so sorry for the way I treat you! You are my only friend, and I don't want you leave me!"

Well, things just worsened. He continued his insane ways with my kids, He started to be very mean to them. I felt so bad that I put them in a situation that caused them to suffer another disappointment. My kids were very nice to him. They used to buy him nice gifts, hoping the presents might make him happy. But this guy was really mean. If you didn't dance to his music, you were not his friend. He was the most difficult person I have ever met. The most horrible thing I heard from his mouth came when he decided to take me out for lunch. As we drove to get lunch, we were just talking about things. Suddenly, he paused for a moment and then said, "I don't know why I can't get what I want!" I asked him, "Like what?" He replied, "I would give a million dollars and do anything to get that person!" I thought, *Oh my gosh! He has a crush on someone!* So I asked, "Who is the lucky one?" He replied, "Oh, you know!" I said, "No I don't. If I knew, I wouldn't be asking you." He says, "Mary." I ask, "Who is that Mary?" He answered, "Your daughter!"

ALL YOU NEED IS THE PLAN,
THE ROAD MAP, AND THE
COURAGE TO PRESS ON TO
YOUR DESTINATION, KNOWING
IN ADVANCE THAT THERE WILL
BE PROBLEMS AND SETBACKS
BUT KNOWING NOTHING ON
EARTH CAN STAND IN THE WAY
OF YOUR PLAN,
BACKUP BY PERSISTENCE
AND DETERMINATION.

I couldn't believe what I had heard. I really lost it. I told him, "I would have expected anybody else except my baby girl! She's my baby! She's only twenty-two years old, and you are forty-nine years old." He said, "She's an adult." I said, "She's my daughter. My daughter is twenty-two years old, but she's like sixteen years old, very innocent." He was very quiet after that. That was the most painful thing he could have said to me. I put up with him for two years, and that was the end of my marriage with him. I helped him with the divorce papers, because I wanted it to end as soon as possible. So, three weeks later, we were divorced. Once again, I had the tools to overcome this nightmare because of my ongoing work in personal development, and my closeness to God has helped me to overcome that mental abuse quickly. What I went through also gave me the opportunity to know about my weaknesses and my strengths and to know that God loves me. He gave me strength, knowledge, and wisdom so I would never fall down on my face again! I didn't even know that I had that much strength. I surprised myself with the great strength that was given to me. After we were divorced, I moved out of his home. Later, I found out that his home had been foreclosed on. From my point of view, he got what he wished for; he used to hate his house and always complained about his neighbors. I don't know where he is now.

What I learned in these relationships was that I married for the wrong reasons. When I married the first time, it was because I didn't want to be alone; I was trying to fill the emptiness that I always had. Unconsciously, I was trying to find the father I never had. Can you understand what I mean? The need for my father's love was so important to me, I even married a guy just like him: alcoholic and lazy. The only difference was that I didn't get beaten physically,

In my second marriage, I was trying to find a daddy for my children. I wanted my kids to have a father they could look up to. I didn't want them to grow up without a father, like I had. My third marriage was for the same reason: a desperate need to give to my children a father. I strongly recommend not getting married to give your children a daddy, mommy, or for money, because you will surely be miserable.

DECIDE TO BECOME A PART OF THE SOLUTION INSTEAD OF PART OF THE PROBLEM.

I felt I needed to be responsible for the choices that I made. This is why I decided to work on forgiveness. I needed to get rid of the hate and anger that was within me, especially toward my first husband. I cannot say that I love God and hate humanity. I understand that God created every living thing. And I also know that God doesn't look at the color of our skin; he looks in our heart!

DO YOU KNOW THE COLOR OF YOUR HEART?

The Promise

God promised us if we do our part, He will do his part!

He says, "My chosen ones, I will lead you to the Promised Land, the land of milk and honey."

For me, I like to think that land of milk and honey is the United States of America.

It is also for many others who came here before and after me. They came with big dreams and goals. They came over the ocean, in the sky, on the highway, and some of them put their lives at risk. But that didn't matter, because their dreams and goals were bigger than their fears. They had one purpose and one goal, which was to get to the United States of America, the land of freedom, opportunity, and abundance.

TO LIVE THE AMERICAN DREAM! FAITH IS OPPOSITE OF FEAR. "FEAR NOT, FOR I AM WITH YOU!" GOD'S ASSURANCE TO US. WE ARE THE MASTER OF OUR FATE, CAPTAIN OF OUR SOUL, AND THE ARCHITECT OF OUR DESTINY!

BECOME A SPONGE FOR
INFORMATION THAT WILL
HELP YOU ON YOUR WAY.
YOU DON'T HAVE TO WASTE
YEARS MAKING
THE MISTAKES OTHERS
HAVE MADE BEFORE.

Unconditional Love

Have you ever had a vision of being reborn in love?
To love is to believe in God, and self-love is the first step to world peace.
Show your children the love you feel, as they are unable to feel your love.
A smile, a hug, a gentle touch, passion, and caring, it means so much.
We live alone for so long, a lifetime.
To live in unconditional love is to never be alone.
Because loneliness is only our perception.
If we trust and let go, it is a new beginning.
With God, I can see what I mean to me.
Life is so beautiful.
Do you know how to love?
Give yourself a second, a third, a fourth chance.
Take another glance at who you really are.
Is it you, or who you think you are?
Did you ever look at yourself in the mirror?

Did you notice how beautiful, important, and special you really are?
You are love.
How can you say you're not okay if you haven't taken the time to look inside your heart and feel; to feel is to heal? Acknowledge that critical voice and tell it to go away.
It's time to play.
Life is short, so don't waste another day!

Sandy Money

HEALTH IS NEVER TO BE
ATTAINED BY STUDYING AND
THINKING ABOUT DISEASE.

We have many challenges in our lives. It's part of being alive on this beautiful planet Earth and how we become strong. If we are prepared, there is no challenge that we can't overcome. But it takes work, like anything else. The only time we will not have any challenges is when we are six feet underground. For me, there are only two ways we can live life: in misery or in happiness. Where you put your time and energy determines what you will reap. Many people get stuck in the, "Why me?" syndrome. I was one of them, too! These individuals think that they are doing everything right, but they know there is something missing; however, they don't know what. These feelings are deeply buried but never forgotten. I know and understand, because I have been there. It's a mind game, what we experience from our childhood, beginning in the womb. What we learned from zero to seven years old is engraved on our brain. Our brain is like computer chip: it saves everything good and bad, where it stays until we decide to reprogram.

Even if you had a great childhood, you may have experienced something painful somewhere along your life's journey. Most people carry deep scars. I know, because I was one of them. I used to carry a deep scar within me. For a long time, I felt like a clown, smiling on the outside but crying on the inside. I don't know if you have noticed other people, but many look so sad, and some of them are angry at the world, because they feel insignificant. So they do something bad. They join a gang or put a gun to someone's head; now they feel significant! Some of them hide their pain by abusing illegal or legal drugs, such as prescription drugs, alcohol, and other things. Why is that? Is it because they want to have an unhealthy life? No, it is because their flesh is weak.

Many people spend thousands of dollars on facelifts and tummy tucks. What about a spiritual facelift? Your spirit is crying for something bigger than you, but you are so busy with worldly things that you have no time to feed your spirit. That is why you are not strong enough to face the real world. Decide to be unselfish by choosing a healthy and productive life. It is the only way you can make a difference in the world. Who is in control, you or the addiction? Did you give away your freedom? Find the power within, find the treasure in your heart. We all have a treasure in our heart; we just forgot or were somehow distracted. Take a look inside your heart and find your power within.

I am very grateful for the great teachers God blessed me with and with the desire to make that change. There is a saying, "If the student is ready, the teacher will appear." Oh boy, was I ready! I was starving for knowledge. Without an empowering education, I wouldn't have been able to write this book. I highly believe in personal development education, because it helped me know about myself, where I was, what I needed to do to become a more productive human being, and what things I needed to know to get where I want to be. I saw that what I was doing was working against me, which is why I looked for an outside source to help me see my internal source of power, find the power within, and build my self-esteem.

RIGHTEOUSNESS IS NOT PROMOTED BY STUDYING AND THINKING ABOUT SIN.

Self-Esteem

Self-esteem is what we think about ourselves in relation to other people. It is the basic secret of our success or failure. First, you have to have an understanding of why we feel lousy about ourselves. What really causes low self-worth? Is it from being constantly criticized by others, bullied by peers, getting consistent, negative reinforcement from others or ourselves, or by blaming ourselves for the abuse we receive from others? It could come from believing the negative things that people say to or about us. The great news is that we can choose how we feel.

When I was growing up, other kids would make fun of me, especially for being an orphan and homeless. It affected me for a long time. When I was a kid, I never had a little friend to play with; the only friends I had were the crickets and the big ants. I remember tying a little string onto my friendly cricket's leg, so my cricket friend wouldn't leave me! I used to be extremely shy and would hardly speak out. Extremely poor self-esteem will do that to you! Everything was working against me. Then I found out that I was responsible for my own feelings. So I started working on myself to become a better person for the people with whom I came in contact. It was, and is, very important to me to become a much better human being.

I learned these words of Eleanor Roosevelt, which make so much sense:

"No one can make you feel inferior without your permission."

Take a look at yourself in the mirror and make that change!

NO ONE EVER GOT
RICH BY *STUDYING*
POVERTY AND THINKING
ABOUT POVERTY.
IF YOU WANT TO
BECOME RICH,
YOU MUST NOT
STUDY POVERTY.

It is important to make the greatest desire in your life. Some people let the past pull them back, acting like it is gravity. Take advice from your mistakes or life experiences and carry on to the future. Don't be like those who live in the darkness of the past, living in the discouragement of the past, and living in the mistakes of the past. Because they didn't make it, and that affects them for the rest of their living lives. We don't want or need the past to pull us back.

Dreams and goals can be magnets: the stronger the goals, the higher the purpose, the more powerful the object makes a stronger magnet that pulls you in that direction. The desire for your dream and goal can pull you through all kinds of upsetting days. We need to change our mind-set from a failure consciousness to success consciousness. One of the common causes of failure is getting into a habit of quitting when one is overtaken by a temporary defeat. One of the main weaknesses of people is how most think about the word "impossible." They know all the rules that will not work for them, and they know all the things that cannot be done! Desire and followthrough are the starting points of all achievement, which means the first step toward success.

> "UNLESS YOU CHANGE HOW YOU ARE, YOU WILL ALWAYS HAVE WHAT YOU GOT."
>
> JIM ROHN

Things to Know Before You Say, "I Do"

Making a stronger marriage

What are the best parts of your relationship?
What would you like to see improved?
What is the best thing about your partner?
What does your partner love most about you?

Below are questions to ensure that both of you are on the same path.

What city would you live in?

Children

Who will stay at home with the children?
If you are unable to conceive, will you adopt?
Is this okay with you?
Will you have a nanny?

What tasks would you expect your
    spouse to be responsible for?
What religion (if any) would they be raised in?
How often would the family attend church services?

Daily activities

Who will cook dinner?
How often will the family eat fast food?
Who will do the dishes?
Who will do the laundry?
Who will do most of the cleaning?
Who will be responsible for lawn care?

General interests

If you gained weight, would this be
    okay with your spouse?
If your spouse gained weight, would
    this be okay with you?
What activities would you do together as a couple?

Health

For health treatments, will you follow Western
    medicine or alternative solutions?
Would your children be vaccinated?

Pets

Would you own any pets?
Who will walk them?
Who will bathe them?

Who will clean up after them?

Tough questions

On what grounds would you separate?
What reason would bring you to participate in divorce?
Do you believe in fidelity?
What if your partner has been unfaithful?
When would you find it acceptable to be unfaithful?
Would you prefer honesty or secrecy
    when it comes to infidelity?

The last questions

What do you expect from your spouse
    in terms of the relationship?
What would you like them to do on
    a daily or weekly basis?
How would you like them to treat you?
Be as specific as possible.
What will you do when the honeymoon is over?

    No other legal contract can be broken so easily. Be responsible; don't be a part of the divorce society. Divorce is painful, you do not bounce back quickly, and the children are the silent victims.

    Before I was married, I didn't know any of these things. I had no education in relationships. Thank goodness I do now!

Choose to make right. Do everything you can to avoid being part of the divorce epidemic! After you say, "I do," wait at least two to five years before you decide to bring children into the world. Give yourself a chance to bond with each other. It is worth it!

Your Health

Healthy eating and exercise is the key to a healthier, happier life.

No person may enjoy everlasting success without good health. Overeating, along with negative thoughts, lack of physical activity, and an inadequate supply of fresh air due to poor breathing techniques, is not conducive to good health. A balanced food intake will help you stay healthy. Include foods such as whole-grains, fruits, and organic vegetables; organic foods are better, since they have no pesticides. Fish, flax oil, spirulina, chlorella, wheatgrass powder, and raw organic coconut are just a few of the delicious foods available. You can go online to get more information and get educated about what you are eating. I believe if we are not learning, we are dying, because this is why we are here on this great planet Earth: to learn. Be responsible for your body, and you can learn about how some foods will help you stay healthy—and some foods will kill you.

Why are there so many obese people? Why don't you take charge when it comes to taking care of your own body? You, no one else, are responsible for the way you want to look. No one is forcing you to eat unhealthy food! Even our little dog Bandit (a chihuahua) likes to eat healthfully; he loves his fruits and vegetables, especially carrots and cantaloupes. I see people drinking lots of soda pop instead of water. I know people who hardly ever eat foods that are healthy for them. They are hooked on prescription drugs. Why? Because they are stupid? No! Because they are simply irresponsible, and the sad part is that if Mom and Dad are obese, the kids are more likely to be obese as well. Not all of them but most of them, because most illnesses are caused by what we eat and the lifestyle we live.

In my opinion, obesity is 80 percent unhealthy eating habits and maybe 20 percent medical causes. Choose the type of food that will improve your health, and avoid the types of food that raise your risk for illnesses such as heart problems and diabetes, as well as lowered self-esteem. I don't know about you, but when I was obese, my self-esteem was in the ground. However, I was not going to stay there, feeling miserable, for the rest of my life. I found out that exercise is the best key to build self-esteem and it may help to conquer depression. Exercise also helps you feel good and have high energy! Women, if you are feeling down, have low energy levels, body aches, and are dragging every morning, I suggest you may want see a medical doctor to get tested. Have your hormone levels tested and find out if your thyroid is working properly. Men, be sure to get your testosterone level tested as well.

My kids and I are very health conscious. When they were little, I used to grow wheatgrass and juiced it every morning. They drank it before they went to school, and were seldom ever sick. When I was obese, I didn't like the way I looked; I had to lose weight! So I took action by changing the way I ate. I also obtained a gym membership. I went to work out at six o'clock in the morning, five days a week. It was not easy, but the results were great. Not only did I lose weight, but it really helped with my emotional challenges. Instead of going to a doctor to get antidepressants and cover the real problem, I went to the gym, where it helped me to focus on positive things and cleared my mind. I also introduced the gym to my kids when they were very young, and now that they are adults, they love to look good!

My son Bryan took me for a vacation, just the two of us, for a whole week. We went to a place called the Optimum Health Institute, located in San Diego. That place is amazing! I really love that place. Everything is so healthy. Everything we ate was raw. I learned so much about eating healthfully. I loved drinking my wheatgrass juice every morning and night. I didn't want to leave, but my son had to be home, because his music album was being released. All of my children have above-average thinking ability. Bryan, Michael, and Mary have great health habits. They eat healthy foods and work out. Bryan eats extremely healthfully, works out hard, and feeds his mind with great books. He is an extremely talented guitarist and is always looking for ways to grow mentally, physically, and spiritually. He is one of my heroes. I admire his desire to want to fly with the eagles! He knows there is no limit when you have a desire to succeed.

> By the way your body looks, I can tell you what you are eating
> **You are what you eat!**

> God, life-empowering seminars, CDs, books, exercise, and love for my children helped me overcome my depression.

To achieve your dreams, you have to decide on what you want and work toward achieving them. You must avoid negative sources, people, places, things, and habits. Believe in yourself, consider things from every angle, don't give up, don't give in, and know that family and friends are hidden treasures. Hang onto your dreams. Ignore those who try to discourage you; keep trying, no matter how hard it seems, as it will get easier and easier. Love yourself, have integrity, and never lie, cheat, or steal. Always strike a fair deal, be committed to succeed in anything that you do, and don't quit, because quitters never win and winners never quit. Read, study, and learn about everything that will play a major role in helping you on your journey. Take control of your own destiny, and don't blame others for your circumstances. Understand yourself in order to better understand others. You are unique of all God's creations, and nothing in this world can replace you!

When I was going through my toughest times, I used to blame others for my unhappiness, I had the victim attitude that no one liked me, and I was not good enough. Sure, I was very angry at the world! It took a lot of work to get to where I am now, and I am very grateful for the transformation I went through. I always believed that if we make ourselves a better person, we will be able to add value to our country. So, with those thoughts in mind, I worked on myself constantly. I am always looking for ways to become mentally, emotionally, spiritually, physically, and financially successful.

I always believed in the American dream: anyone can become financially free if they choose to. With that belief, I bought my first business, a hot dog truck, which I later sold because the business was not doing well. Next, I opened a gift shop in one the casinos in downtown Las Vegas. But the casino went bankrupt, so I lost that business. I did not lose my faith, because I don't have a "give up" attitude. So I bought another business, a deli. It was very tough to run the business and raise three kids.

I was not able to find a competent babysitter and had to make a decision between kids or the restaurant business. So I sold the business and went back to school. I wanted to be a nurse, so I tried it for one year, but I didn't like what I saw at a nursing home. So I went to cosmetology school. I really liked it, and I finished the school very fast and went to work at one of the local hair salons. I worked in that profession for many years. Then one day, I asked myself, "Is this it? Is this what the American dream is all about?" I knew there had to be more, because I felt like I was traveling through a dark tunnel, trying to find the light. Besides my regular job, I sold lotions, potions, and vitamins—among other things—but I was still struggling financially.

I was always looking out for new opportunities. I always kept my options open and never had a closed mind. Later, I decided to open a beauty salon business. I bought all the equipment and started looking for a location, but something was telling me that there was something else out there for me. Since I was always on the lookout for other opportunities, the opportunity found me! The most mind-transforming business: network marketing! The amazing part of the network marketing business is that the system is already in place to win; the other amazing part is that it came with a personal mentor.

The business costs a very small amount to get started; what a sweet deal. The beauty salon was going to cost me between $60,000 and $80,000, and I would have to work from sunup to sundown without a personal mentor. It would give me the privilege to make my own schedule. I would have more time and freedom for my family, which was very important to me. The most amazing part was that it would allow me for personal growth. I called the university with a check ready. How did this business find me? One day someone gave me a business card, actually two business cards. On the card it said "Home-Based Business Opportunity." I liked that word—"opportunity"—so, a couple weeks later, I called the number on the card, but no one answered. I called the other number on the other card. This time, I got an answer. He said, "Hello, this is Al Thomas." I said, "Hi! This is Sandy, and I heard about the business opportunity and would like to hear more about it." He said to meet him at one of the coffee shops, so I got the pleasure to meet him. He gave me the business presentation, and the rest is history.

I didn't understand anything. The only things I saw were a lot of dollar signs! I didn't ask for identification or say, "Let me do my research." I signed up right on the spot. I didn't want to miss my opportunity. The only thing I wondered about was if I could do it. That was the first time I ever met a multi-millionaire. Al Thomas was willing to mentor me and teach me how to get where he was. He said, "I am going to teach you step-by-step what I did to get where I am today." I was so excited, because no one had ever spoken to me like that. I was thinking, *He's going to charge me a lot of money to mentor me.* I asked him, "How much would it cost to be mentored by you?"

"Nothing!" he said. "The most important thing is that you succeed financially, so you can do the something for other people, help others to succeed like you did." Wow! I could not believe what I was hearing! Then he gave me the *Rich Dad, Poor Dad* CD by Robert Kiyosaki, my first CD, my first lesson on how rich people think and how poor people struggle. He also suggested books to read, such as *Think and Grow Rich*, for my first year in network marketing.

After we finished the meeting, I told him, "Bye," and then ran to my car to pop the CD into the player to hear what kind of message there was for me. It blew away my mind. This is the first time I ever learned how rich people think and how poor people struggle because of the way they think. The more I listened to the CD, the more I realized that I was in the poor-people thinking category. I used to beat myself up, because I thought since I didn't have a college degree, I wasn't good enough. I could never be rich, so I would just have to settle on being an average person. With that in mind, I used to push my kids to get good grades. I used to tell them to get good grades, so they could go to college and find a good company to work for with benefits. The more I pressured my kids about good grades, the more they rebelled.

I grew up thinking that if you didn't have a college degree, you were nobody. After listening to the CD, however, I came to realize that I was not done yet. I still have had a chance for financial success. That was great news for me, and it can be for you, too! I believe money is important; money buys freedom and makes life more enjoyable. The more money we have, the more value we can add to other people's lives. Money is up there with oxygen, people say money doesn't buy happiness, but neither does being broke. They say that money is the root of all evil. I say no. The *love* of money is the root of evil.

Well, we already know how poor people think. Go to school, get good grades, and go to school again. Find a good company to work for—one with benefits—work for forty years, and retire broke. Maybe in some other country it is okay, but not here in America.

Rich people know that when you go to the bank to ask for a loan, the bank doesn't ask for a school report; they ask for a financial report. That was something new to me. Rich people believe that they create their lives; poor people believe that life happens to them. Rich people think that financial education is more important, and working in a team is more important than working alone. Most schools do not teach those concepts. Schools think if you work in a team, you are cheating. This was something else I had never realized. I was so shocked at all the things that I was missing, and the things that I was hearing were really mind-transforming. There is no way in the world I could have learned on my own without this CD. Thank you, Mr. Al Thomas, for giving me my first CD, so I could reprogram my financial thinking.

Another thing that I like is Robert Kiyosaki's teaching. He says that the poor work for money, and the rich make their money work for them. This is something else the school system doesn't teach. How can they teach us about wealth, when the teachers live paycheck to paycheck, and if you fail your grades, they say that you are stupid and will never make it in anything? Those types of words kill the kids' spirit and can lead to high dropout rates. Many teachers don't know the impact their words have on a young mind.

This is the first time I learned about residual income, which means you work once and you get paid over and over again.

The Two great entrepreneurs, Robert Kiyosaki and Donald Trump, Mr. Trump believes strongly in direct sales marketing, which is why he endorses ACN; he believes in what this company has to offer. Robert Kiyosaki and Mr. Trump wrote a book, *Why We Want You to Be Rich*. It is a great book; I read it from cover to cover. They both strongly believe in financial education, because it is how they became very successful in their businesses. They ask why is money important? Money buys freedom, and success is the choice.

They strongly recommend the network marketing or direct sales industry; it is also known as multilevel marketing (MLM). In my opinion, it should be called the human development industry, because average people have the opportunity to own a company within the company. They train people to win by teaching you to become business owners. It involves great personal development, and that's why I call it personal development with a compensation plan. I wish schools were like that; maybe more kids would stay in school. It's about having more control about your life by making more money. In your job, you have no control; your boss or company decides how much you are worth.

If you own a small business, the reality is the business owns you. I know, because I have been there. Network marketing also teaches teamwork by getting along with other people. Most people have the "I'll do it myself" attitude. In reality, we need each other. Some people shy away from network marketing and say they are not a good salesperson. The truth is that we have been selling ourselves since we were born. If you wanted your bottle, you would cry and your mom would give you a bottle of milk. And when you're at the dating age, you dress up and hang out where the single people are. So what are you doing? You are selling yourself! When you are looking for a job, you tell all the good things about yourself so you can get that job. You are selling yourself! You've been selling yourself all your life, but you just didn't know it!

Some skeptics say, "Oh, it is a pyramid scheme. I don't like it, because it's a pyramid." In reality, they've probably been part of a pyramid for most of their life. For example, in the school system, the hierarchy is principal, vice principal, assisting office workers, and teachers, and so forth. The pyramid as it relates to your job may consist of the president, vice president, manager, and assistant manager. Your boss is way up high, and you are way down on the bottom, where the little guy has a slim chance to get to the top!

I think fear keeps people from trying something new. But in network marketing, mentors will teach you how to overcome your fears, because fear is crippling. If you allow fear to take over, you will not have a winning mentality. But if you have the desire, they will help you develop your leadership abilities. In network marketing, you invest a small amount, but the compensation is unlimited. You decide how high you want to go, and everything is there for you to succeed—great support personnel and business. The plan was created for average people with a success mentality to build an empire in the company. You work for yourself but not by yourself; it is designed to bring you to the top and not keep you at the bottom like your job.

The only thing that you have to bring with you is a winning attitude, the ability to take action, vision, belief, faith, work ethic, passion, tenacity, high motivation, integrity, and a code of honor, and you must be coachable. These are the power tools you need to bring with you. Do you remember when a franchise came out forty years ago? People thought franchises were bad; doubters said they would never make it big. But look at them now. How big are they, McDonald's, Wendy's, Carl's Jr., and KFC? One day I heard my friend, a hairstylist, complaining about her financial situation; she was almost crying, and I really felt sad for her. I tried to help by suggesting a solution. I asked her, "Why don't you try something else part time while you are working as a hairstylist?" Her answer was, "I don't want to. I love doing hair! I've been doing hair for over twenty years, and I am hoping that I can meet a nice man with money." I was very surprised by her answer. She's in her fifties, okay! I asked her what was wrong with her ability to make more money, she said she didn't know.

That reminds me of when my mentor told me, "Sandy, many people do the same thing over and over again, and they expect to get different results. That is the definition of insanity! They are afraid to take risks, and they look for a job." The most important thing for them is job security; they conform to living paycheck to paycheck and live a mediocre life. I tell you, find a reputable network marketing company and work around your schedule. Give yourself three to five, even ten years, and watch for that residual income. You will be glad you did. You will reap what you sow. This business is not an overnight success; it is not a get rich quick scam. It takes time, and it is up to you how slow or fast you want to succeed.

The only way you can fail in this business is if your pride and ego get in the way. Those are the only things that might stop you from succeeding. To change yourself is to change the map of your reality. Focusing on what you want is more useful than focusing on what you don't want, as our focus determines the direction we will go, where our energy and resource will be spent. There is no such thing as failure. The only feedback all experiences provide is the opportunity to gain wisdom. If our behavior gets the results we want, we have learned what works. If we don't get the results we want, we have learned what doesn't work. We learn from experience, and there is no such thing as failure.

The only desire I had when I started in the network marketing (MLM) business was to become very successful, make money, and get promoted in different positions very fast. Guess what happened to me? The big fat fear took over me. The fear of success! In all my education, there are two things that I missed out on:

1. How to invest my money and who am I going to help with my money. I had no plan for how I was going to manage my money, so I was becoming very successful, but the fear of success overtook me. I said to myself, "Oh my gosh! I'm getting successful so fast! Oh no! The challenge is not going to be there anymore!" Guess what happened to me? My success was taken away from me and went to someone who was ready for a successful blessing. At that time, I didn't know what I was doing to myself, so I continued doing the business but with much more struggle than before. I say to you, "Don't do what I did." The most important thing that you can ask yourself is why you want to start your own business and why you want

to become financially free. Why do you want to make money? What are you going to do with the money? Who are you going to help with the money you are going to make? Know why you want to make lots of money or want to be rich. In this business, you will become financially free if you don't quit, because multilevel marketing works if you work at it. You have to be brain dead not to be able to understand how simple it is to run your multilevel marketing business. Believe in yourself and have faith that you deserve to live the American dream. Don't let anyone steal your dreams!

2. My financial blueprint was not yet programmed, and I didn't even know that there was such a thing. One day I went to a seminar called "The Millionaire Mind." In that seminar, I learned the roots of how some people are successful in whatever they do and how some people struggle financially all their lives. Donald Trump, Bill Gates, Warren Buffet, Robert Kiyosaki, Michael Jordan, Tiger Woods, and all others who have reached a high level of financial success are there because their financial blueprint is set up for financial success. As for average people, their financial blueprint is set up for a life struggle. You see, our financial blueprint is like a fruit tree. What happens if we plant the fruit seeds in good soil, water, and fertilizer and then take good care of the fruit tree? The fruit tree will produce great fruit. Are you getting it? Okay, our mind is like the roots of that tree, and the fruit is our financial success.

Our financial blueprint is subject to the way we were conditioned when we were growing up. When I was growing up, there was always a struggle about money. I heard people say money is evil, and rich people are evil, greedy, exploit their workers, and steal from the poor. You can never be rich, because it is very hard to be rich. Poor people are humble and don't have problems like the rich do; money is filthy and doesn't buy happiness. Can you see? I was conditioned with a very negative perspective toward money. If that is how people have been conditioned about money, how can we attract financial success when our thoughts and feelings about money are negative?

The seminar was amazing! I learned that if I wanted to become financially successful, I must reprogram the way I think about money. We need to set our thermostats for success—like wealthy people do. It's very important to admire rich and successful people. If we resent them, we are setting ourselves up to fail. How can we be something that we dislike? Rich people see opportunities, poor people see obstacles; rich people see potential growth, poor people see potential loss; rich people focus on rewards, and poor people focus on risks. Rich people expect to succeed. They have confidence in their ability and creativity, and they believe that they can always find a way to reach their goals. Rich people are willing to take on big responsibilities; that's why they are rich. Average people run from responsibilities, and that's why they're broke. The good news is that your financial blueprint can be changed. Ask yourself where you are. How is your childhood conditioning affecting your finances now? Identify and change your personal financial and success blueprint forever. Recognize your money personality; learn to build on your strengths and overcome your weaknesses. Use spiritual laws to create real world success.

> "Your income can only grow to
> the extent that you do!"
>
> -T. Harv Eker-

I was also amazed to learn how our little voice talks to us, you know that monkey chatter in our mind? Are "recession," "inflation," "deflation," and "depression" economic terms or our little voice's terms? We hear, "It's rough out there," yet I've also heard many times this is when many people will be very wealthy. "The weak don't survive when it comes to winning." It's all about our little voice. Rather than letting deflation, depression, and recession become us, we need to learn to convert those terms into prosperity.

Abundance and power need to be in all areas of our life—financially, emotionally, spiritually, and physically. We need to learn how world champions master their self-esteem and self-discipline to live healthy lives and make lots of money. It is surprising how our thoughts program us for success or mediocrity. Our words can rocket us to success or failure. Determine what you really want and motivate yourself to get started, keep going, and most important, finish what you started. Be careful! The part that wants us to stay the same is not always our friend. It tells us not to change, to keep things the way they are, feel like a victim, and on and on. When we follow that monkey chatter, it keeps us unhappy and stuck. Yet, we still follow it! We drop the ball on our life, we pick fights with people we love, we play victim and feel sorry for ourselves. No one really wants to come to our pity party. When we serve up huge doses of self-pity, it costs us our dreams when we wait and drop our agreements. We forget that we really are magnificent creators.

> "I do not think there is any other quality so essential to success of any kind as the quality of perseverance. It overcomes almost everything, even nature."
>
> ~John D. Rockefeller~

When I came to the realization about me being the master of my fate, captain of my soul, and architect of my destiny, I was amazed. I had always thought that circumstances or something outside of me was in charge. Knowing all that, I'm more excited to work on myself. I don't have any excuses to blame someone else about my destiny. I know that self-mastering is the hardest job you and I will ever tackle. If we do not conquer self, we will be conquered by self. We may see at one end at the same time, both are our best friend and our greatest enemy by stepping in front of a mirror.

Before I started my emotional transformation, I often struggled with limiting beliefs. Our beliefs limit us from being able to create the future that we want. Your beliefs can take you to success or failure. We make decisions that create beliefs, and they run throughout our lives. What beliefs did you create in the past that are limiting you from getting what you want right now? Do you understand that if you believe it is not okay for you to have a successful relationship—with someone who is absolutely perfect for you—and that perfect person walks into your life, you may never notice him or her, because you will be waiting for the relationship you're going to fail.

Money was probably one of the biggest challenges that I had to face, as I was raised with the limiting belief that it isn't okay for you to make a lot of money and that money is the root of evil. If that describes you, too, the most incredible opportunity for financial freedom may come your way, but you will probably miss it, because you are looking for what won't work. You would be looking in all the wrong places. Perhaps you decided in the past that it wasn't okay for you to have a lot of money. I know some people have the opportunity to make more money but they refuse! I think that is being ungrateful and that they are rejecting their blessing and the opportunity to grow financially. They say, "It's okay. I don't want to make more money. I have just enough to get me by." I say to them, "If you don't want to make more money for yourself, why don't you make more money and give it away?"

We live in the United States. It is impossible for you to not want to make more money. Even Donald Trump wants to make more money. Why? All the extra money he makes is donated to charities. He enjoys helping others, and besides, he has more money than he could ever spend in a lifetime. What's keeping you from making more money? Are you limiting your beliefs? What is your financial blueprint, and how is it formed?

Thoughts lead to feelings.

Feelings lead to actions. Actions lead to results.

Your financial blueprint consists of a combination of your thoughts, feelings, and actions in the area of money. So how is your money blueprint formed? The answer is simple: your financial blueprint consists primarily of the information or programming you received in the past, especially as a young child. Who was the primary source of this programming or conditioning?

For most people, the list includes parents, siblings, friends, teachers, and media. Did you ever hear of phrases like, "Money is the root of all evil," "Rich people are greedy," "Rich people are criminals," "Filthy rich," "You have to work hard to make money," "You have to have college degree to make a good money," "Money doesn't grow on trees," "You can't be rich and be spiritual," "Money doesn't buy happiness," "The rich get richer, and the poor gets poorer"? Ninety-five percent of people think this way. No wonder ninety-five percent of people are broke and five percent are financially free! My mentor always told me that the bottom is too crowded, but the top feels great, because it's not too crowded. There is plenty of room for those who want to get to the top!

Money is not the root of all evil; it is the love of money. Rich people are not greedy; rich people are generous look at Donald Trump, Warren Buffett, Anthony Robbins, and many other wealthy people. They donate a lot of money to charities. I never met any rich people who were filthy; they are very clean and wear nice outfits. They don't have to work hard physically to make money. They work smart. Money doesn't buy happiness? Being broke can't buy happiness either! Money is up there with oxygen. When you were born, did you decide that you will be broke, a slow learner, helpless, lazy, stubborn, have bad luck, that others wouldn't like you, or that you were not good enough? What you want to do right now is to clear out those things that are keeping you limited. You are magnificent, you are God's creation, and he does not create junk!

What about our emotions?

Negative emotion blocks the flow of positive energy in the body as well as the real possibility of creating a functional blockage in the nervous system. Trapped emotions could actually cause the brain to send a wrong signal (or no signal at all) to the various organs in the body. That means there are emotions in the body that we haven't let go of. Not only can they be a source of discomfort, they can be the source of other physical problems, such as a heart attack. When do you think most people suffer a heart attack? Monday morning! Negative emotion blocks the flow of success and keeps us from achieving our goals. How many times has anger gotten in your way when you wanted to communicate something to someone? Think about a time when you felt angry. Did you say, "Oh gee, this feels great. I hope I can continue to feel this way all day?" No, of course not! Some people do anything to break up the feeling of sadness, including sleep, immerse themselves in work, exercise, go to a movie, or talk to a friend—anything to keep from feeling the bad feelings. Negative emotions can lead people to smoke, drink alcohol, overeat, abuse others, take drugs, and much more. You can take control over your beliefs to power your unconsciousness: the freeway to change your conscious and unconscious portion. Your consciousness is the part of your mind that analyzes, criticizes, and thinks logically all day long. It is where your attention is located. Your unconsciousness is the part of your mind where all your memories are stored; it's your memory bank.

Did you ever have an identity conflict? I did. I didn't know who I was or where I belonged. It felt like I was lost spiritually. Did you ever ask yourself who you really are? Who you are defines your identity. Are you a leader or follower? Are you the one who makes a difference, or are you a victim? Your life is defined by you. Do you believe you are your past or are you who you decide to be now? Who are you? You are a miracle, you are a gift to the world, and you wore born to win! The most amazing feeling is when you really find your identity with your creator. That happens when you really connect spiritually with God! Try it. You will feel what I mean.

BIRTH…….....……LIFE……….....……DEATH

What you do between is what counts!

"I never had a crisis that didn't make me stronger."

If you want to make the world a better place, take a look at yourself in the mirror and make that change!

When you were little, you had no control of the way you were treated by your parents or others. But now you are an adult. You are in control of you, your thoughts, your feelings, your actions. You are in control, and no one else has control over you!

You are responsible for choosing which path you are going to take from now on. Failure or success is up to you, and no one dictates your future except you! It doesn't matter what you did in the past. What matters is what you are going to do from now on.

Don't let other people make your choices for you.

Choose your friends. Who you spend time with is who you become. You cannot scratch with turkeys if you want fly with eagles.

Stay away from people who put you down or treat you badly. Remember, vampires suck your blood, and negative people suck your energy!

Be your own best friend, love yourself, and remember that you are a special miracle and a gift to this world.

Be true to yourself and your values; be honest with yourself and others.

Respect other people and treat them right.

Have faith; faith is the opposite of fear. For me, my faith in God helped me overcome my fears.

Set goals and work to achieve them. Don't quit, because quitters never win and winners never quit.

You are born to win; to be a winner, you must plan to win and expect to win!

God be with you.

Much love,
Sandy Money

"People with goals succeed because they know where they are going … it's as simple as that."
~Earl Nightingale~

"Don't let what you cannot do interfere with what you can do."
~ John Wooden ~

"It takes a lot of courage to show your dreams to someone else."
~ Erma Bombeck ~

"It is in your moment of decision that your destiny is shaped."
~ Anthony Robbins ~

"Always bear in mind that your own resolution to succeed is more important than any other thing."
~ Abraham Lincoln ~

"Never leave that till tomorrow
which you can do today."
~ Benjamin Franklin ~

"Concentrate: put all your eggs in one
basket, and watch that basket."
~ Andrew Carnegie ~

"You must do the things you
think you cannot do."
~ Eleanor Roosevelt ~

The poor need inspiration. Charity only sends
Them a loaf of bread to keep
them alive for a day;
But inspiration will cause them to rise out
Of their misery.

Because you are not in the right business
or the right environment now,
don't think that you must postpone action
until you get into the right
business or environment.
After you have obtained a hope in
Christ, you shall obtain riches,
if you seek them; and you will seek them
for the intent to do good to clothe
the naked, to feed the hungry, to
liberate the captive, and administer
relief to the sick and the afflicted.
Jacob 2:19

Peace I leave with you, my
piece I gave unto you.
Let not your heart be troubled
Neither let it be afraid.
John 14:27

Cast thy burden upon the Lord,
And he shall sustain you.
Psalm 55:22

Every day is either a successful day or a
day of failure; it is the successful day
Which gets you what you want

When the man is all together,
His world is all together.

Suggested Readings

Why We Want You to Be Rich
by Donald Trump and Robert Kiyosaki

Secrets of the Millionaire Mind
by T. Harv Eker

Think and Grow Rich
by Napoleon Hill

The Science of Getting Rich
by Wallace D. Wattles

Attitude 101
by John C. Maxwell

Feelings Buried Alive Never Die …
by Karol K. Truman

Conquer Fear
by Lisa Jimenez

For more information visit
www.powerwithinlifecoach.com